God Said it

365 Times in

the Bible; DO

NOT BE

AFRAID.

God said 365 Times in the Bible; DO NOT BE AFRAID.

Series "Spiritual Attraction "
By: Sherry Lee
Version 1.1 ~February 2023
Published by Sherry Lee at KDP
Copyright ©2023 by Sherry Lee. All rights reserved.

All information in this book has been carefully researched and checked for factual accuracy. However, the author and publisher make no warranty, express or implied, that the information contained herein is appropriate for every individual, situation, or purpose and assume no responsibility for errors or omissions.

The reader assumes the risk and full responsibility for all actions. The author will not be held responsible for any loss or damage, whether consequential, incidental, special, or otherwise, that may result from the information presented in this book.

All images are free for use or purchased from stock photo sites or royalty-free for commercial use. I have relied on my own observations as well as many different sources for this book, and I have done my best to check facts and give credit where it is due. In the event that any material is used without proper permission, please contact me so that the oversight can be corrected.

TABLE OF CONTENTS.

INTRODUCTION.

They were horrified, exclaimed, "It's a ghost," and shouted out in fear, but Jesus quickly said, "Be of good cheer! It is I. Don't be frightened." Matthew 14:26a-b and 27 NIV.

One of the many exceptional qualities of our Lord is that He doesn't permit His children to dwell in their worries. In the context of the verse cited above, when their anxieties were clear, He responded instantly with ".Don't be afraid." He did not wait until they were completely afraid before revealing who He was. Instead, the text reads, ".Jesus said instantly to them."

God is not pleased when His children are paralyzed by fear. The Bible is filled with evidence pointing in the opposite direction. **IT IS STATED THAT THE BIBLE HAS 365 TIMES THE PHRASE "FEAR NOT," ONE FOR EACH DAY OF THE YEAR.**

Now, not all worries are dangerous and paralyzing. For instance:

Fear of harming an infant compels you to handle him with the utmost care and tenderness.

The fear of harming your body prevents you from touching a hot stove.

The surgeon operates on his patient with the utmost precision and cares out of a healthy concern that he might endanger the life entrusted to his care at that moment.

However, irrational worries stem from a lack of faith in God's power to assist us. These worries enslave us and often prevent us from performing the many good acts we could do for others in the name of our Lord. These are the anxieties that render us dysfunctional.

Furthermore, fear may lead us to sin. Therefore, trust is essential for combating fear. For example, if I am in difficulties and I don't trust God to aid me, I will rely on speaking a lie for help. Then, I seek refuge in a lie and reject God, who is the Truth.

Moreover, if we sincerely feel that God loves us, we will trust Him more readily because it is much simpler to trust someone who loves us. Therefore, it is written: "In love, there is no fear." May our eyes be awakened to the boundless love the Father has for us, for then we will have greater faith in Him and no fear.

You are no longer required to live in fear because God states "Fear not" 365 times in the Bible. This life-changing book will assist you in overcoming your worries and beginning a life filled with peace, joy, and hope.

Have a pleasant reading experience.

CHAPTER 1: DOES FEAR RULE YOUR LIFE?

When we fear, worry, or stress over anything, we are genuinely under its power; that emotion governs us. God has also shown me how often and easily our enemies attack us. The other day, while watching a commercial for a particular product on television, I got the unsettling thought, "I'd better do something before it's too late." Immediately, the Holy Spirit declared, "This is that fear.

Are you going to make me your Lord or the enemy?" Fear, anxiety, and tension originate from the enemy. God doesn't want us to experience the fear, anxiety, and stress the world constantly throws us.

We are the ones who allow fear to govern our lives. What does God say, and what has He bestowed upon us?

"Peace I leave with you. My peace I give you; not as the world gives, I give you peace. Let your heart neither be worried nor terrified." John 14:27 Because God has not given us the spirit of fear but love, power, and a clear mind. 7th chapter of Second Timothy

He has already endowed us with a spirit of strength, love, and sanity. This is already present within us. In other words, don't allow yourselves to worry, stress or be afraid of anything! This world attempts to provide us with peace, safety, and security in different ways, but the only true and perfect peace comes from God.

If you are putting God first in your life, I can guarantee that the devil will attempt to instill fear and confusion. When we entertain these thoughts, they can seize control of us, but with the power of God, we are the ones in charge. The goal is not to allow that concept to penetrate.

When these concerns take control, we attempt to handle things independently. God vehemently opposes our doing this! Jesus has accomplished so much for us via his crucifixion and resurrection - not simply salvation, as I've highlighted in earlier writings. He desires us to let go of our loads, fears, worries, and anxieties - Jesus bore these for us on the cross so that we may immediately live in HIS grace, power, boldness, joy, love, and peace!

He desires that we reach the point of, "I've tried, but I'm powerless - Lord, please take control of all aspect of my life. Permit me to complete your requests promptly and at your convenience." I recall a day when I returned to God on my deathbed.

I surrendered everything and placed my entire trust and life in His hands. It's incredible how easily things can creep back in! We can attempt to cling to things so tightly, despite His constant reminders, "I adore you so much, so don't be afraid, don't stress, and don't worry!

You are irreplaceable to me. You are my most cherished and favored child. My feelings and thoughts for you are much greater than any love you've ever experienced.

Why can't you let go and have faith in me? You don't have to be constantly weighed down by these burdens. It makes my heart ache. Permit me to possess your heart and preserve it because I love you. I wish to be the love you have never known." Listen to His voice and His heart.

As the Holy Spirit told me, I had to choose between submitting to the enemy or the Lord. Wouldn't you rather experience God's perfect peace, joy, love, and power? He is awaiting your arrival, but the decision is yours.

This makes sense to my mind. I am a firm believer in God's kingdom. Thus, this is my path to attain it. Renewing my thoughts is how and where this process begins. When the mind is at peace, so are the spirit, soul, and body.

CHAPTER 2: IS THERE ANY REASON TO FEAR?

An old proverb states, "There is nothing to fear except fear itself." This is a clever statement that is entertaining to believe. However, there are things to fear other than fear itself, God.

Who are enlightened?

Who are those who are brimming with knowledge?

Is it those who have an extensive understanding of global affairs?

Men's hearts will fail them out of fear and anticipation of upcoming events, for the heavenly forces will be shaken. Because the Bible states, "Fear God," a man with true wisdom fears God.

1 Corinthians 3:19 Because the world's wisdom is foolishness in God's eyes. Because it is stated, He

catches the wise in their own cunning. Man's folly stems from his ignorance of God and misunderstanding of his environment.

Man's fear (A painful emotion or passion produced by the expectancy of evil or the fear of approaching danger.) has departed from God. Still, it has increased due to worldly concerns, money, power, position, war, and death.

Mankind is terrified of death, the big unknown. Is it because they are carnally minded and believe in an afterlife? Is it because, although they claim not to believe, they secretly pray that there is no God?

There is no trouble convincing people that Heaven exists, but that Hell exists is a different story. Many so-called teachers of the Gospel assert that the biblical descriptions of Hell and eternal punishment are allegories, references, and illusions for something else.

The search for a treatment for heart disease will be fruitless, as anxiety and worry are major contributors to heart attacks. This worry results from strain from your job, house, family, finances, and life's inherent uncertainties.

Deuteronomy 32:6 Do you thus repay the LORD, ignorant and unwise people? Is he not thy father who purchased thee? Hast thou not been created and formed by him? Many don't fear God; even those who kill in God's name don't fear His vengeance for their wrongdoings. What do we say to God when we claim, "You did not create me?"

1Timothy 5:20 Those who sin should be rebuked in front of everyone so that others may also be afraid. We must stand up for God's word and be determined to defend the Good News of Jesus Christ.

When others teach erroneous doctrine, we reprimand them harshly and openly, causing others of a similar mindset to fear spreading lies out of hypocrisy. We reduce not a single word from God's message, for the sent word will achieve what it was intended to do.

This fear is a reverent fear of God, replaced by those who have strayed from the gospel's truth and their fear of God. If we lose this reverent fear, we walk aimlessly and become susceptible to every wind and ideology that blows our way.

The fear of death as well as the fear of man have driven many to melancholy and a gradual withdrawal from society and the Gospel. This fear originates from Satan and is employed to torment the unsaved and those with weak faith. Often, this fear leads to suicides and murders.

Hebrews 13:6 So, we may confidently say, "The Lord is my helper, and I won't fear what man can do to me." Man utilizes fear as a weapon against man. Satan also employs fear as a weapon against humans.

Fear is a dominating force that devours the mind, body, and soul. It is comparable to cancer in that it eats away at the basic fabric of the human body until it controls and destroys the will to live.

"The Lord is my help;" Believing in God and His Son Jesus is the finest approach to regulate and guard against fear because you can't know God without both. We, as believers, possess a power many don't recognize or don't utilize. What is this ability?

The Power of Christ's and God's Spirits, who dwell within us. Acts 1:8 "But ye shall receive power when the Holy Spirit has come upon you; and ye shall be my witnesses in Jerusalem and all of Judaea and Samaria and to the ends of the earth."

Luke 10:18-20: "And he said to them, I saw Satan fall from heaven like lightning."

Behold, I bestow upon you the ability to tread on serpents and scorpions and all the power of your adversary (Satan, all unrighteousness, demons of darkness): nothing shall ever harm you.

Despite this, don't rejoice that the spirits are subject to you; instead, rejoice that your names are written in heaven."

Ezekiel 2:6 And thou, son of man, have no fear of them, nor be terrified of their words, though briers and thorns are with thee and thou dwellest among scorpions: have no fear of their words, nor be alarmed by their looks, even though they are a rebellious house.

What should we fear?

The body fears pain and suffering, the mind of the flesh fears death, but the spirit is fearless so long as we serve the creator of all things. Your spirit will choose your fate; it will choose between right and wrong. Good and evil. Life and death.

Fear has no place in the spirit of a Christian; thus, it doesn't control his or her life. Fear originates from Satan, stems from uncertainty, and produces anguish. We must remember: "The Lord is my helper; I won't be afraid of anything a man can do to me."

In these latter times; Luke 21:25-26; And there shall be signs in the sun, in the moon and the stars; and upon the earth distress of nations, with perplexity; the sea and the waves roaring; Men's hearts failing them for fear and for looking forward to those things that are coming upon the earth: for the powers of heaven shall be shaken.

The night sky displays different views of humanity. Many assert that these lights and objects are extraterrestrial aliens observing and studying Earth. This is the fulfillment of the prophecy "And there shall be signs in the sun, in the moon and the stars," which states, "And there shall be signs in the sun, in the moon and the stars."

According to 1st Corinthians 15:34 "Awaken to righteousness and don't sin; for some don't have God's wisdom; I say this to your shame." With God's wisdom, there is no confusion, uncertainty, misunderstanding, or fear. However, many lack an understanding of God.

This results in many forms of creativity, awe, and minds that seek knowledge but find none. God considers man's knowledge and wisdom foolish because man's knowledge is restricted to the material and not the spiritual.

2 Peter 2:9 The Lord knows how to deliver the righteous from temptations and reserve the unjust for punishment on the Day of Judgment. Remember the saying, "There is nothing to fear but fear itself." There is nothing to fear other than being in God's wrath hands.

CHAPTER 3: CONFRONTING YOUR FEARS.

Fear is one of the most difficult difficulties most people face. Fear is one of the colossi that constantly destroy our potential. Fear, however, has been described as a small trickle of uncertainty that rushes through the mind until it wears such a large channel that all your ideas drain into it. This worry continues daily until we are miserable and can't function.

It focuses on what could go wrong rather than what could go right. Although accidents occur and cars must be properly maintained and driven, the fear that prohibits us from driving or riding in a car cripples our potential because it greatly restricts our movement.

Most of the time, believers and nonbelievers cause fear to grip their hearts when they are tormented in multiple ways. To illustrate, the disciples who had Jesus by their side appeared to be in continual fear of storms, crowds, poverty, armies, and the loss of their leader. We may immediately recall the day Jesus instructed them to cross to the other side of the Sea of Galilee.

The night descended like a blanket, a storm sprang out of nowhere, and the disciples fought for their lives as the seas threw the ship. They were afraid to even when they saw Jesus approaching the water. They believed he was a ghost (Matthew 14:22-23). They caused them to be overcome with fright.

Also, when David was a youth, he encountered the enormous Goliath, who preyed on their fear by issuing challenges he knew they would not accept. Fear reigned over King Saul, first of the giant, then of the boy who slew the giant.

This is because he overcame his fear by trusting God rather than focusing on what could go wrong. He liberated the Israelites from their enemies' oppression and revered the name of God (Samuel 17). However, he armed his slingshot with five stones and retreated. It is claimed that courage is not the absence of fear but its mastery; it is the intersection of faith and fear.

You see, the opposite of fear is not courage. It is not faith. Love is the opposite of fear. This verse expresses the beauty and strength of this fact. As Paul wrote to Timothy concerning his ability to overcome fear (2 Timothy 1:6-7), "God has not given us the spirit of fear but of power, of love and a sound mind."

On the other hand, fear is an army of giants because it multiplies one into many. At the same time that it does this, it diminishes us in our own eyes. We lose sight of the promise that we can accomplish all things through him who strengthens us. We can't perceive anything in its true perspective. Fear devours it, not the object of the fear.

Furthermore, there is yet another reason to become involved in ministry. As you can see, my advice to establish a closer relationship with God is not trite. Be an encourager. Be an ambassador of God's love. I am unaware of any superior prescription.

That is the pinnacle of fear tactics. Children experience fears of contacting their parents. It is the same for adults who are fearful, but the parents whose names we call are far more responsive.

You should immediately begin drawing closer to God if your life is riddled with anxiety and illogical anxieties. Increase the time you spend in His Word, invest more time in prayer, and keep a prayer journal detailing how He comforts you in times of fear.

A proverb states, "He who is afraid to try will never know what he could have accomplished." A person who fears God has nothing else to fear. To enhance your life, you must overcome your fears via faith.

Fear not, for I am with you; don't be terrified, for I am your God. I will strengthen you; yes, I will assist and support you with My right hand."

Fear is one of the most terrible emotions and ideas a person may have. It will render you incapacitated and immobilized. It will make you fearful that your current position and life, in general, may take a negative turn.

Someone stated that it is identical to faith in a negative sense. If we have faith, we believe something positive will occur; if we have fear, we believe something negative will occur. The antithesis of faith is fear.

Fear is the assurance of what we fear, but faith is the assurance of what we hope for.

Fear prevents us from taking risks, moving forward, and discovering new ways of doing things.

Fear will compel us to remain where we are. Be satisfied with what we have accomplished. Become ordinary in our lives and shy or unmotivated to try new things.

Without Fear.

Back in the day, the term NO FEAR was used to describe warriors, combatants, athletes, teams, and even businesspeople. "No fear" is a beautiful motto and a useful reminder for all of us, especially those experiencing challenging situations. "No fear" might be of help to those who are battling with insecurity, illness, desertion, and even loneliness.

But NO FEAR also has a side effect. This generation includes children, adolescents, and adults with little respect for authority. Disrespecting elders and authorities, rebelling against the law, and refusing to submit to those we must obey - even God.

This is merely a comment on the phrase's excessive usage. It is the negative connotation or misunderstanding of the statement NO FEAR. A misunderstanding likely led to the incorrect application. The term is positive and uplifting, but if applied outside its intended context, it would cause different problems.

"No Fear" and "Fear Not" may appear to have the same meaning. However, "Fear Not" is more applicable when discussing overcoming fears in our hearts and lives. In this piece, therefore, I offer the phrase "FEAR NOT." God's message to everyone in the Bible is DON'T FEAR. He repeated this over a hundred times to reassure us that He will always be with us and never abandon or forsake us.

Therefore Have No Fear.

God is with us, so fear not. What a magnificent promise from our Creator. Many individuals find it difficult to accept that the God of the universe, the Lord of all the earth, and the most powerful Being is the One who told us NOT TO FEAR because He is always with us. He's our Defender, Provider, Healer, Comforter, and Redeemer.

God is God; have no fear. Even though everyone is against you, nothing else matters if God is on your side. As the Bible states, "a thousand may fall at your side and ten thousand at your right," you should not be scared. People may have misinterpreted you, spoken ill of you, condemned and despised you but know that God is on your side and not against you.

Because nothing is impossible with God, everything is possible! You can encounter mountains of tests, valleys of trials, and other types of storms, but if you trust that God is your God, you will prevail and emerge victorious. You and God are already the majority, the winning team, and nothing is impossible with Him.

Every day has many obstacles. Deadlines, dead ends, workloads, overloads, no cell phone load, bill payments, tuition costs, peer pressures, financial commitments, and relationship issues of a similar nature are all common occurrences. God is your source of strength.

We are weary, exhausted, and worn out. Rest if you are exhausted but don't give up. Know that the Lord is your strength if you are feeble. He will make you strong in your weakness if you learn to approach Him in faith.

God is your help and will hoist you up, so don't be afraid. He is our help in a hopeless circumstance. He is willing to help us when we are in need. He offers help when we believe no one else will. As the Psalmist cried out, "I raise my eyes to the heights; from whence comes my help? My help comes from the Lord, who created heaven and earth."

Dear reader and friend, while you confront different obstacles today, minor or large, I hope you will remember God's promise that He is with and for you. He loves you so greatly that He even conquered death, the most awful foe man could ever face.

Therefore, the next time fear arises, look up with eyes of trust and see God's huge hands reaching toward you, prepared to carry you through. Not to be concerned.

No fear? I disagree since, in truth, we all experience fear, but because we knew and believed that God is larger than our anxieties, we decided not to fear.

CHAPTER 4: ARE THERE ANY BENEFITS OF FEAR?

Fear has diverse meanings for different people. Fear is a drive for certain individuals to accomplish their best. Others are deprived of their greatest performances by evil. Then, what is fear, and why do people discuss it with such hatred?

Before we define fear, let's admit that humans are naturally fearful. Fear is as innate or natural to him as doubt. Fear is the bad or uneasy emotion that emerges in the heart or within a person when they are in danger or when their safety or security is endangered. It is a circumstance in which a person must confront or face ambiguity, negative certainty, or impossibility.

Even though my attempt to explain the word 'fear' may appear inappropriate, everyone knows what fear is and when one is afraid or in fear. The key point, though, is why fear plays such a significant role in human life, and yet, despite the importance of fear to humans, no one is encouraged to live in fear.

According to the Bible, God hates or abhors fear, especially when it manifests in His people or servants. God, His angels, and even Jesus, during His lifetime, are shown in the Bible as speaking to or rebuking His people or servants against fear or being terrified. This is evidence that God hates or detests fear in His people or servants.

In this chapter, I will demonstrate that God doesn't actually or completely condemn individuals for being fearful, regardless of the cause. A single observation stands out in practically all biblical accounts of God's guidance to His people or servants regarding fear or being terrified. "For" is the suffix or other or subsequent word.

When or whenever the Lord says "Fear Not" to a person or individuals, He will add "For." This "For" will convey why He told the individual not to fear. Examples can be found in Isaiah 41:10, 43:1-5, 44:2-3,

Genesis 15:1, Joshua 1:9, and Luke 1:13, among others. As a result, we may see that the Lord detests or abhors fear in or among His people primarily because of what He knows about Himself and the source of their fear.

God is aware that He is always with His people; He will always satisfy their needs, face and conquer the object of their fear or doubt and see them through it. He is also aware that nothing or no one could threaten them and that He could not overcome or vanquish them on their behalf.

He knows He is the creator of all things and beings and controls everything. He is also aware that no emergency exists with Him. He can't be taken by surprise because He knows and sees everything, even the end, from the beginning (Hebrews 4:13; Acts 15:18; Jeremiah 23:24), but He is persuaded that fear is innate or inborn in humans.

Man was developed in this manner. Fear occupies a large portion of him, and in many respects, fear propels him to higher accomplishments; therefore, man must work with and employ fear.

Fear is an effective weapon in human life. Man is continually confronted with the fear of failing or the worry of losing his competitive edge while doing his professional obligations. In daily existence, the man typically realizes that fear drives him to strive for excellence or settle for mediocrity.

The Bible, for example, attests to this truth. Nevertheless, the book of Proverbs describes six human traits that God hates or detests, especially in His people and servants, including FEAR.

It is also true that the frequency with which God warns His people and servants against fear indicates or shows His hatred for it, even though fear assists or saves individuals daily. Fear assisted the Christ-followers in their service to God.

Let us recall that the Bible urged all Christians to have a reverent fear of God, the highest form of fear. We are concerned about disobeying God and living in opposition to His ways out of fear.

According to the Bible, fear of God is the beginning of wisdom (Proverbs 9:10). Fear is reverence for our great God, submitting to His flawless plan, and seeking His living wisdom. We can live sensibly in an unpredictable world by having a proper reverence for God.

God, however, is concerned with the fear that paralyzes human activity - the fear that turns intelligent people into vegetables. Consequently, persons who engage in this fear are neither spared nor praised. They create the God who assures His children of His presence, protection, and help in all circumstances.

With all that the Lord God knows about Himself and His relationship with His people or servants, He considers it a lack of trust or confidence in His person, sincerity, faithfulness, and ability when He observes His people fearing anything or anyone to the point where it prevents them from carrying out their duties. He views it as an insult to His person as well.

God loathes in a man the kind of fear that makes him an easy victim of the object of his fear. Such a fear erodes faith, trust, and courage, leaving the frightened individual at the mercy of the object or individual feared; hence, those who understand the power of fear always employ it against their prey, target, or opponent. When David encountered Goliath in combat, Goliath initially exploited fear as a weapon.

This was one of the secrets to David's success over Goliath, as he was already aware of this fact (1 Samuel 17:41-47). Knowing the power of fear, the devil (Satan) often employs it on his victim or target and succeeds most of the time, as those who are afraid are always his victims.

When he fires or casts fear into a person's heart through some methods, if it is received, it reduces their trust, confidence, courage, and resistance, allowing him to intensify his attack or activities on or against his target, so achieving his purpose or goal.

Fear is natural to humans, but God's people may reject or conquer it because they are no longer subject to the rules of nature but to the laws of the Spirit (Romans 8:1-9; 1 Corinthians 2:14). If we truly comprehend and believe who and what God is and our relationship with Him and everything else related to Him, we will have little or no reason to fear. Whenever fear attempts to manifest itself, we will always oppose it.

CHAPTER 5: WHAT HAS GOD SAID YOU SHOULD DO WHEN AFRAID?

God provides extremely clear instructions on what to do when we are fearful; we should not be afraid! Jesus repeatedly told the multitudes He encountered during His time on earth, "Don't be afraid." Does this imply that as God's offspring, we shall never experience fear? No. The Psalmist said in Psalms 55:5 that he experienced fear and trembling. Just as fear overcame the psalmist, it might also overtake us.

Where does fear originate?

To answer this question, it is crucial to realize that there are two forces in the world, both of which are typically invisible to us: a force for good and a force for evil. These forces are discussed in the Book of Deuteronomy, specifically in chapter 28. God instructs Moses to warn the people that if they obey

His commands, they will experience good fortune, but if they disobey Him, evil will enter their lives.

Let me pause for a moment to emphasize that students of the Bible who correctly divide God's Word will realize that God never tempts people with evil, but evil exists in the world; thus, people must choose to reject evil and follow good.

In Deuteronomy 30:19, God commands and describes the principle of rejecting evil and pursuing virtue. "I call heaven and earth to record this day against you, that I have placed life and death, blessing and cursing, before you; therefore, choose life so that you and your offspring may live."

When someone rejects the Word of God, they expose themselves to evil, and fear will always follow. In Deuteronomy 28:66, God warns us that if we reject His Word for our lives, our lives will hang in the balance, and we will live in constant fear; we will have no certainty of life whatsoever. According to many analyses, the essence of this is that we will live in perpetual anxiety and anticipation of our deaths.

This sounds very much like what so many people are experiencing now, right? Wars and rumors of wars! Look around, and you will see what I mean: the anxiety caused by global economic uncertainty, not to mention the fear that accompanies the morning news and headlines on worldwide turmoil.

Let's return to what God instructs us to do when fear strikes. Psalm 27:1 provides the answer for us: "The LORD is my light and my salvation; whom shall I fear?" The LORD is my life's strength; of whom should I be afraid? In other words, we must have faith in God.

Jesus Christ declared in Matthew 7:24-27 that anyone who hears and does what The Word says to do would be a wise person whose house will be built on a rock and who will endure and overcome the storms of life.

The converse would also be true; anyone who heard what God advises to do and chose not to implement it would be like a fool who builds a house on sand; they would not withstand the storms of life but would be destroyed.

Allow me to ask: Do you have faith in God? If fear rules your life, then the answer is no. If fear is a part of your life, please know that Jesus Christ and His Word offer a way out.

Consider a shadow, which has a form but no substance; similarly, fear possesses a form but no substance; thus, there is no need to be terrified.

According to 2 Timothy 1:7, God has not given us the Spirit of fear but of power, love, and a sound mind. Who has instilled fear if not God? Fear is one of the Devil's primary techniques to keep us in servitude. He is conquered; thus, his only remaining source of strength is mental subjugation, which he pursues. If we allow him, he will maintain our fear of something.

According to the Bible, God, not Satan, created Heaven and Earth; hence He is in charge of everything. He has a plan for everyone, but we can't fulfill it if we dwell in fear.

Fear is a component of the curse, and Jesus has freed us from fear since the Just shall live by faith.

How do we conquer fear?

First, we must put our faith and trust in the Lord, who is full of love and compassion and doesn't want us to perish. He has, therefore, good things in store for us. Nothing we have done can separate us from His love. Therefore, we don't need to engage in self-condemnation and abandon our trust in Him because of our actions.

In this day and age, there may be uncertainty, but we must remember that God has given us Jesus, so how could He not provide us with good things and provide for us via Him? God is, therefore, in control of everything and sends us only wonderful things.

This is a great location because the Lord can demonstrate His strength and save us. If we confront a problem, we should not be afraid but rather tell the Lord about it, and He will offer us comfort and serenity. So often, we will attempt to solve an issue, but there will come a time, possibly now, when there is nothing we can do.

The Lord tells us 365 times to not be afraid. This is because fear is subject to the curse, and we have been liberated from it. God can't intervene on our behalf if there is fear; He moves by faith, and it is impossible to satisfy Him without trust.

Jesus indicated there would be hardship in this world, but He did not tell us to fear it. Instead, He said, "Be of good cheer, for I have overcome the world." Even during difficult circumstances, we should be at peace because He has given us His peace. His Peace will keep us alive.

The Bible certainly foretells awful events that will occur on the planet but also instructs us to look up because our redemption is nigh. Jesus provides salvation for all of our needs; He has never failed, so we should not permit ourselves to be afraid. Once we surrender our fears to Him, we shall be liberated from their shackles.

CHAPTER 6: COMMUNICATING WITH GOD - THE IMPORTANCE OF FAITH.

Faith is necessary to communicate with God. There are different ways we could define faith, but its essence is belief. Even more so, we may say that faith is belief.

I will use a text from Hebrews to define faith as it relates to talking with God.

Genesis 11:6 But without faith, it is impossible to satisfy him, for he who comes to God must believe that he exists and that he rewards those who seek him with diligence. (KJV)

This verse illustrates that trust in God entails believing in God's existence and a conviction that God rewards those seeking him.

Consider for a moment your communication with your best friend.

Before communication can begin, there are a few things you must believe. First, you must believe in the existence of your friend; otherwise, what would be the sense of communicating?

Second, you must believe there is some benefit to communicating with that person. The reward may be as simple as expressing your emotions and feeling understood.

Both beliefs are essential to developing communication.

So let's now broaden our thinking and explore interacting with God.

You must first believe that God exists.

For many individuals, this is irrelevant. If you are reading this, you likely believe in God's existence. If you are reading this and don't believe in God, congratulations on your open mind! I am not attempting to persuade anyone of anything, so please enjoy the reading!

Having faith to believe that God rewards those who seek Him is essential.

I believe this because many of us have been taught that God should be feared. This God is kind and merciful but occasionally jealous and cruel. Let's face it: we've been taught that if we don't fly properly, we'll be condemned to hell after we die, which is not exactly a notion consistent with being rewarded for pursuing God, right?

We prefer to focus on the side of God that damns souls to endless hellfire, which, let's face it, is terrifying as hell.

If you live in fear of a God who punishes and sends people to hell, can you believe he rewards those who seek him?

You say that's what you believe, but why are you so terrified? Why do you have so much doubt and fear? Why do you sense such a disconnect with God? Why do you feel God doesn't hear you?

This dilemma appears to be among the most fundamental spiritual issues. The authors of the Bible endured it. Read some of King David's writings; he seems to have experienced a roller coaster connection with God.

How do you feel?

It appears pertinent that Jesus remarked, "Fear not, little flock, for it is your Father's delight to give you the kingdom."

Take your "fear thermometer"; if it's elevated, you're not truly living by faith in God as a reward for those seeking Him.

Consider what you are terrified of. Is it an unnecessary fear? You'll most of the time discover that it hasn't occurred - it doesn't even exist!

Why would you desire to reside there?

Wouldn't it be more desirable and reassuring to believe God rewards people seeking Him?

If you adopt this stance, you will find yourself craving constant communion with God.

CHAPTER 7: HOW TO CONQUER YOUR FEARS WITH THE HELP OF GOD.

Living in fear is debilitating and contrary to God's will for our lives. "For God has not given us a spirit of fear but of power, love, and a clear mind," the Bible says." 2 Timothy 1:7 (NKJV) "Meaning that God doesn't want us to experience any form of fear. Whether it is a fear of public speaking, trying something new, or reading the Bible, it is not from God. As a Christian, you are capable of conquering your fears.

To live in perfect surrender to God, we must conquer the fear in our life. Jesus died not just for our sins but also so that we may have abundant life. A life devoid of fear is abundant. When we live in fear, we demonstrate an absence of faith.

Our worries, if powerful enough, can cause terrible outcomes in our lives, as they did for Job: "For that which I feared has come upon me and what I feared has occurred." Job 3:25 (NKJV). There are strategies for overcoming the fear that will result in a deeper peace in Christ Jesus.

Step 1: Recognize Your Fear.

You must recognize your anxieties and their underlying reasons. Some root issues are not as readily apparent or identifiable on the surface. Ask yourself questions to determine the source of the issue. For instance, queries such as what is fear?

What is frightening you, and what does it remind you of? When did you first become aware of this fear? Is this a legitimate concern for a follower of Jesus Christ? These questions must be answered before proceeding with the other steps.

Step 2: Read the Bible.

The Bible has advice for overcoming any obstacle in our lives. Specifically, the Bible instructs us not to be afraid of anyone or anything. Reading the Bible will assist you in overcoming fear in your life. Whom shall I fear, since the Lord is my light and salvation? asks Psalm 27:1.

Find biblical passages proclaiming God's omnipotence and Jesus' lordship as our savior. Construct trust in the belief that God is who he claims to be and will accomplish everything he has promised for your life.

Step 3: Meditate.

When you discover verses that rebuke your fearful thoughts, ponder on them. Meditation consists of reflecting on thoughts and mentally repeating phrases or principles. The benefits of meditation can diminish our fear.

The more you focus your mind and spirit on the power of Christ Jesus, the less fear you will feel. Consider anything that GOD HAS ALREADY DONE for you in which the outcome may have been considerably worse.

Remind yourself that God has a plan for your life in Jeremiah 29:11: "For I know the plans I have for you," says the LORD, "plans to prosper you and not to harm you, plans to give you hope and a future" (NIV). What is there to fear if God's purpose for your life is good and without harm?

Step 4: Pray.

You can never pray too often or too fervently about a personal matter. Everything begins and concludes with prayer. When we face difficulties in life, we must bring them to Jesus. Fear can be eliminated from our life if we have faith in our prayers. Even fear can be moved or vanquished through earnest and intense prayer in this life.

Fear is an oppressive spirit for a Christian. Christians must combat fear by discovering its core cause, reading the Bible, meditating, and praying. Fear, like any other habit or spirit that wants to impede our walk with Jesus, must be overcome. Fear will go when we are ready to truly understand who God is in our life and the ultimate sacrifice Jesus made for us.

On the cross, Jesus' love for us has already conquered fear. However, our love for Jesus will eradicate all fear from our life. "There is no fear in love, but perfect love extinguishes fear because fear causes suffering. Fearful individuals are not made perfect in love " (1 john 4:18).

CHAPTER 8; GOD'S WAY TO OBTAIN VICTORY OVER FEAR.

First, let's determine where fear originates. Hebrews 2:14-15 states, "Since then the children partake of flesh and blood, he (Jesus) also himself likewise took part of the same; that through death he might destroy him who had the power of death, that is, the devil; and deliver those who had been subject to servitude for their entire lives out of fear of death."

The basis of all fear, therefore, is the fear of death. According to Deuteronomy 28:66, fear is a curse of the law, but according to Galatians 3:13, Jesus Christ freed you from the curse of the law. Therefore, you are no longer subject to fear.

If you are a Christian, Jesus' death on the cross has given you victory over death and the fear of death. How thankful we are to God, who gives us victory over sin and death through our Lord Jesus Christ (1 Corinthians 15:57)! Fear of God should be the only fear a Christian should ever experience.

Thoughts, beliefs, words, deeds, and the law of sowing and reaping are five things that, when employed appropriately, can help you develop an inner picture of courage devoid of fear. How well you grasp these five elements will influence how you navigate life.

Let's examine how God would have you approach these five things to overcome any unwarranted fear and replace it with a positive, courageous inner image that conforms to Christ's image.

Your goal should be to conform to the image of Christ because your genuine identity can only be found in Christ. "For whom he foreknew, he also predestined to be conformed to the image of his Son, so that he might be the firstborn among many brothers" (Romans 8:29).

1. THOUGHTS - Your beliefs are determined by your thoughts. What you say is determined by your beliefs.

What you say will determine your behavior, which will determine your life's trajectory. "He is as he thinks within his heart" (Proverbs 23:7)

To develop a positive inner image conformed to the image of Christ, God wants you to think and focus on things that generate a successful and courageous image within you. "Finally, brothers, if there is any virtue and if there is any praise, think on these things" (Philippians 4:8).

2. BELIEFS - Yes, your thoughts can become your beliefs. Ensure that your thoughts will result in a pleasant belief system in God. Create a new set of positive self-beliefs by reflecting on and communicating God's promises about you.

Set aside time daily to boldly express what God has said about you. This will begin to dismantle false beliefs. The faster the outcomes, the more time you devote to renewing your mind with the Word of God.

"Therefore, I implore you, brothers, by the compassion of God, to present your bodies as a living sacrifice, holy and pleasing to God; this is your proper worship. "And don't be conformed to this world but be converted by the renewing of your mind, so that you can test what is the good, pleasing and perfect will of God" (Romans 12:1,2).

Assuming you are a Christian, you can begin pondering and boldly proclaiming the following truths about yourself immediately. These declarations will assist you in forming a new, positive inner belief system based on God's Word:

In Christ, I am victorious, an overcomer, triumphant, more than a conqueror, faithful, justified, anointed, blessed, holy, dead to sin, have all power, forgiven, loving, humble, gentle, a saint, light of the world, chosen, beloved of God the Father, seated in heavenly places with Christ, God's workmanship, have peace, have joy, secure, protected, thankful, all my needs and wants are met, have the wisdom and mind of Christ, right

According to 2 Timothy 1:7, God has not given me a spirit of fear but of power, love, and a sound mind.

According to Isaiah 54:17, no weapon fashioned against me will succeed.

As you reflect on, consider, and repeat the affirmations above, you will eventually come to believe them and manifest them in your life. Your inner image will be conformed to Christ's image. Therefore, destroy false beliefs (mental strongholds) by contemplating and expressing God's Word.

For the tools of our fight are not carnal but powerful through God for the destruction of strongholds; casting down imaginations and every lofty thing that exalts itself against the knowledge of God and bringing every thought into captivity to the obedience of Christ (2 Corinthians 10:4-5).

3. WORDS - Words are effective. "And God said, Let there be light and light appeared" (Genesis 1:3). "The tongue has the power of life and death and those who love it shall eat its fruit" (Proverbs 18:21). What you ultimately say will reflect your beliefs.

"For with the heart a man believes to righteousness, and with the lips, he confesses to salvation" (Romans 10:10). "Because we share the same spirit of faith, as it is written, I believed, and so I spoke; we also believe, and so we speak" (2 Corinthians 4:13).

Words create "images" within your mind. Words spoken often can build an internal positive or negative image, depending on the words spoken. If you continually speak negatively about yourself, you will construct a false, negative image of yourself within yourself. A negative image might become a fortress in your life that must be destroyed. Strongholds can induce fear and a sense of inferiority.

Start demolishing any negative image strongholds in your mind by speaking God's Word (His promises), which will paint a positive, prosperous, and victorious image on the inside of you, an image that conforms to the image of Christ. "Therefore, if someone is in Christ, he is a new creation; the old has passed away; behold, all things have become new" (2 Corinthians 5:17).

God desires that you guard your tongue and speak only what you desire to come to pass. Start speaking life rather than death. Speak the solution (God's wonderful promises) rather than the issue. According to 2 Peter 1:4, you share in the divine character of God under His promises. His promises illuminate your identity in Christ. "Set a guard, O Lord, before my mouth; guard the entrance to my mouth" (Psalm 141:3).

4. ACTIONS - Everything you think, believe, and say will eventually manifest in your actions. You will also act adversely if you have bad thoughts, beliefs, and speech. Now, let's reverse the curse and have you begin to think, believe, speak, and act following God's Word.

Think, believe, and utter the wonderful promises of God that reveal who you are in Christ: "Therefore we have been given exceedingly large and precious promises, that ye might share of the divine nature, having escaped the corruption that is in the world through lust" (1 Peter 1:4). (2 Peter 1:4).

As you do so, your inner image will morph into that of Jesus Christ, the universe's most successful, loving, intellectual, and wise person. You have been redeemed from the curse, and you are now blessed.

"Christ rescued us from the law's curse by becoming a curse in our place; for it is stated, Cursed is everyone hung on a tree. So that the blessing of Abraham might come onto the Gentiles through Jesus Christ and that we might receive the promise of the Spirit through faith" (Galatians 3:13,14).

5. Sowing and Reaping - You will harvest what you sow. You sow a seed when you contribute tithes (one-tenth of your monthly income). "Don't be fooled; God is not amused; whatever a man sows, he will also reap" (Galatians 6:7). A financial seed seeded via faith possesses extraordinary power.

This levy, your financial seed, cares for the House of God (your local church where you attend). In return, God provides a harvest that covers your household expenses. You label your giving seed when you sow (give) an offering that exceeds your tithe. What you call your offering affects your yield.

Let me clarify. You desire a victorious inner image. You would name your gift seed "Inner Image of Victory." You would then thank, praise and worship God daily until your harvest of a victorious inner image presented itself. Even though the "Sowing and Reaping" website focuses on finances, the sowing and reaping theory applies to all areas of life, including cultivating a good self-image.

As stated previously, the powerful principle of sowing and reaping can be applied to every aspect of your life: weight reduction, peace, financial wealth, a holy life, victory over sin, joy, a repaired marriage, physical healing, inner confidence or anything else in keeping with God's Word that you desire.

Jesus stated, "If you love me, you will obey my commands." Mark 16:15 commands us to share the gospel with the lost. Please don't be a disobedient Christian and forfeit the soul-winning crown that awaits you in heaven.

CHAPTER 9: KEYS TO ERADICATING FEAR.

Faith expands. This is what Jesus taught when He compared faith to a seed. As it expands, faith also grows stronger. Undoubtedly, you would agree that a seedling is weaker than a 100-year-old oak. When acorns and maple seeds germinate in my yard, I have no trouble removing them, but if I allow them to continue growing, I will require muscle and power tools to pull them out or cut them down.

The same holds for irrational fears. Fears that have been ingrained were not addressed when they initially arose. If you allow them to take root, they are far more difficult to remove. The more fear dominates your life, the less power you have over it.

If you've ever seen ivy climbing a building, you know it has a firm grasp on the underlying bricks and cement. Given sufficient time, it can demolish the structure. If you've ever attempted to pull down and eliminate ivy, you know it isn't easy. Both the tendrils and roots are well-rooted and difficult to eliminate.

In the southern United States, a vine known as Kudzu can destroy anything and rapidly colonize the land. Its high growth rate robs other plants of light, water, and nutrients. Similar to fear, it is intrusive, pervasive, and persistent.

Fear is deceptive. Satan begins with small things, such as a fear of snakes, flying, or public speaking. If he can make you fear one thing, he can spread that fear to other areas of your life, like tentacles.

Fear is also restrictive. It prevents you from expressing or doing what you should or desire. Often, the devil uses other individuals to maintain your fear. You ask yourself, "What do 'they' think?" Then, you psychologically and occasionally physically withdraw from the perceived threat. You forget God's care and encouragement to face and overcome your worries. You forget His assurances of strength, power, stability, and victory.

Fear is Satan's most powerful weapon and may halt you. Fear entangles you in defeat, reliance, and despair. It is a mentally and spiritually harmful weed. It will penetrate, suffocate and ultimately kill your religion, just like that Kudzu vine did.

God wants His people to be fearless! Fear not, for I am with you; don't be afraid, for I am your God. I will strengthen you, aid you; I will support you with the right hand of My righteousness (Isaiah. 41:10).

You must eliminate all fear to receive the benefit and blessing of His strength, help, and support. Here are five methods to overcoming your anxieties and bolstering your trust.

Incline - Listen to my words, my son; incline your ear to my words. Keep the words in the center of your heart and don't let them from thy sight (Proverbs 4:20-21). Incline signifies favorable disposition or willingness. It is also a hilly terrain. Spending more time in God's Word will strengthen your faith. Incorporate His wisdom into your thoughts so that you "fear not and believe exclusively."

Casting down imaginations and everything that exalts itself against the knowledge of God and bringing every thought into captivity to the obedience of Christ. (2 Corinthians 10:5) Refuse means to decline. It also signifies a constant and progressive decline of strength. A person with deteriorating health becomes weaker. Send your fears downward by refusing to acknowledge them in your thoughts.

Align - Be vigilant; remain steadfast in the faith; conduct yourselves as men; be strong (I Corinthians 16:33). To align is to set or position something, to straighten or provide support.

Align yourself with what God has said about you, what He had promised you, and the strength He has bestowed upon you. As you agree with His Word concerning yourself and your circumstances, fear will be eliminated from your thoughts and speech.

For those of us who have faith, rest comes. Therefore, let us work to reach that rest, lest anybody follow the same path of unbelief (Hebrews 4:3, 11). You enter

God's rest when you lean toward His promises, reject thoughts of fear or disbelief and align yourself with His Word. You are relaxed and at ease when reclining, not anxious, tense, and afraid.

Rejoice - Rejoice always in the Lord; again, I repeat, "Rejoice!" Worry about nothing but in everything, via prayer and petition with thanksgiving, make your requests known to God; the peace of God, which surpasses all understanding, will guard your hearts and minds in Christ Jesus (Philippians 4:4, 6-7).

God stated that you can be confident that He always hears your prayers AND grants your requests. There is no reason for worry if you are resting (reclining) in God and trusting His promises. Replace fear with gratitude and adoration, reveling in His goodness.

Fear, anxiety, tension, and stress should be added to your list of negative thoughts. Fear is an omnipresent and pervasive mental weed. Fear is also the greatest adversary of faith, yet it can be destroyed and eradicated with constant, determined effort. If you incline, decline, align, and recline, you will soon be able to declare, "My life is perfect!"

CHAPTER 10: CONFRONTING YOUR FEAR IS THE KEY TO HAPPINESS!

We overlooked a critical point in our emphasis on discovering and fulfilling your God-given destiny in life and relationships. Your fate and relationship fulfillment depend on the thing you fear the most. Your fate and relationship fulfillment depend on the thing you fear the most. Please repeat the statement.

Our life purpose and relationships are most likely related to our greatest fears! Due to this it may be why we waver between staying where we are and pursuing our desire for something better with what we have. Could your worst fear prevent you from experiencing a higher quality of life?

Consider Moses. Most would agree that Moses' objective was to free the Israelites from Egypt. Recall that Moses rescued his Hebrew sibling from the Egyptians. Moses ultimately killed the Egyptians.

Pharaoh attempted to murder Moses after learning of his act. Moses, we are informed, fled in fear for his life. For 40 years, Moses wandered in the desert. He married Zippora and worked alongside Jethro, his father-in-law, during this time.

Eventually, Moses observed a burning bush whose branches remained uncharged. God had the opportunity to speak with Moses because Moses was curious about this reality. God informed Moses that He had heard His people's cries for help in Egypt.

The people of God desired freedom. God informed Moses of His intention to deliver them. Furthermore, He was giving Moses the mission. Years earlier, Moses demonstrated a propensity to do precisely this when he rescued an Israelite brother from an Egyptian.

Moses was still terrified. He provided some excuses for why he could not do this project due to his fear. Moses was doubtful of himself and dubious of God's support. Neither Pharaoh nor God's people believed him, and he had poor communication skills.

When these efforts failed to sway God's mind, Moses told God to send another messenger! This made God angry. Still, God did not relent. Aaron was tasked with accompanying Moses. God would converse with Moses. Moses would converse with Aaron, and Aaron would address Pharaoh and the Israelites.

Intriguingly, Moses did not reveal why he did not want to return to Egypt in his lengthy list of excuses. However, Moses' unwillingness to return was the precise reason he fled! He was terrified. Moses feared that Pharaoh would recall his vow to murder him.

Moses was terrified for his life! Although Moses did not convey his anxiety to God, God answered Moses' fear by informing him that those who had wanted to kill him had been eliminated. Read Exodus 4:19,

The Lord told Moses in Midian, "Return to Egypt; all those who sought your life [for killing the Egyptian] are dead."

God reassured Moses by stating that all who wanted his life had died. In other words, he no longer needed to worry about them. All these years later, Moses's mistrust of men remained unresolved. God addressed Moses's main anxiety upon requesting that Moses return to Egypt to deliver his people.

Still, Moses had to have faith in God, return to Egypt, and confront the personification of his fear, Pharaoh, to experience full freedom and achieve his destiny! This portion of the tale of Moses is recorded in Exodus 2-4.

Moses' heroic deeds, which resulted in the liberation of Israel's children, are justly lauded, as they led to their liberation. Nevertheless, I maintain that this was not Moses' greatest victory. Moses's greatest achievement may have been conquering his fears! Ten times did Moses overcome his fear of (Pharaoh's) authority! He confronted Pharaoh ten times with miracles and plagues.

We ponder why it took ten conflicts to fulfill God's desire. God declared that He would harden Pharaoh's heart so he would not release the Israelites. Exodus 4:21 reads,

The LORD then said to Moses, "When you return to Egypt, be sure to perform all the miracles I have given you before Pharaoh, but I will harden his heart, preventing him from releasing the people.

Wait a minute! Did you read the previous passage? God will harden the heart of Pharaoh. This indicates that Pharaoh would have promptly complied. God would prohibit Pharaoh from granting Moses' request! But if it was God's wish for the Israelites to be liberated, why would He prevent it from happening ten times? What would this achieve, and who would it benefit?

It helps Moses overcome his apprehension of confrontation. The more he confronted his fears, the more confident he got. Ten times he tried and succeeded! I assume that following the ninth triumph,

Moses' attitude and determination to confront Pharaoh were drastically changed.

Consider his spirit and goal in this manner. Suppose you summon your children downstairs. The first two times, your child disregards you. The third and fourth time, he or she responds, "Okay, I'll be there."

The fifth time you call someone by their first and middle names. However, he or she doesn't arrive. The sixth and seventh time you call your child's first, middle and last name and command him or her to come. However, they don't come. He or she fails to appear.

The eighth and ninth times you use all their names, you present them with a request. If there is still no response, you approach the individual and bring them to the desired location. You have only done what you have done. Consider what you are experiencing mentally and emotionally. You become annoyed, furious, and more insistent.

Finally, you take steps to ensure that your request won't be denied. With each request and non-response, your spirit and intent become stronger. By the tenth time, you, your child, and everyone within hearing distance know you are serious. Right?

If Moses was uncertain of himself when he left Midian, he must have arrived in Egypt still unproven and uncertain! Even if just in his mind, Moses may have needed to pass ten tests to be considered authentic.

This was the most essential and unaccounted-for intellect. Pharaoh had to be prevented from granting Moses' initial request. God had already decided that Moses would be chosen. Moses was the only person who doubted he was the one! Thus, it is possible that Moses benefited from the miracles and plagues as much as anybody else.

Regardless, assigning greatness based on outcomes is simple, but the genuine, awe-inspiring truth of greatness lies in the obstacles one must overcome to perform such heroic acts. This is true in marriage, family, community, church, and global relationships.

Everyone has greatness within. As was the case with Moses, this implies that you and I must confront our fears! There is no alternative! As long as we are willing to confront our greatest fears, nothing can prevent us from realizing our destiny and forming intimately satisfying relationships!

The realization that we must confront and overcome fear to achieve happiness and fulfillment in life and relationships eliminates any need to brag about our accomplishments. It is God's mind-boggling, ego-defeating wisdom to disguise our greatest accomplishments within our biggest fears. Matthew 17:20 indicates:

Jesus said, "Because of your disbelief; for I tell you, if you have faith as small as a mustard seed, you will say to this mountain, 'Move from here to there,' and it will move; and nothing will be difficult for you."

CHAPTER 11: HAVE NO FEAR; I WILL ASSIST YOU!

Who will pay attention to this? Who will attempt to hear and read these words? In the middle of today's plagues - depression, economic collapse, global recession, earthquakes, tsunami, wars, ethnic and religious strife, diseases such as cancer and Ebola, etc. - are you afraid? In the middle of all the suffering, anguish, and misfortune, will you now give up?

These prophecies have been predicted to manifest as the world's end approaches: "You will hear of conflicts and war rumors; take care not to be alarmed or distressed, for this must occur, but the end is not yet.

"For nation will rise against nation (Palestine and Israel clash where thousands of both innocent and sinful souls have been swallowed up by the earth) and kingdom against kingdom, and there will be famine and earthquakes in place after place; All these are merely the beginning of the labor pains. " (Matthew 24:6–8), and fear, sadness, and despair have already taken hold of the hearts of the world's inhabitants.

As children of God (real believers), the Lord's peace must remain in our hearts regardless of the chaos and tragedy. "God did not give us the spirit of fear but of strength, love, and a sound mind" (2 Timothy 1:7) so that we may endure the storms of modern life.

Daily, we read of murders, assassinations, rapes, fear-related effects, suicides, and other sufferings. Still, I assure you that "the Angel of the Lord encamps around those who fear Him" (Psalm 34:7). "Fear not because of evildoers, for they will soon be cut down like grass and wither like a plant. Trust in the Lord and do good; then you will dwell in the land, feed on His faithfulness, and be fed in truth " (Psalm 37:1-3).

"The Lord is aware of the days of the righteous and blameless, and their legacy will endure forever. They won't be put to shame in times of calamity, and they will be satisfied in times of famine." (Psalm 37:18-19).

"Behold, God is your helper and ally; the Lord is 'your' upholder (through trials). He will repay evil to 'your' foes; and in His faithfulness, He will put a stop to them for you" (Psalm 54:4-5).

Simply "throw your weight upon the Lord, and He will uphold you; He will never allow the righteous to be shaken" When you put everything before the Lord and submit to His will, He becomes "your Rock and Salvation; your Defense and Fortress and you shall not be shaken" (Psalm 62:6), regardless of the severity of the storms or the pressure of your enemies.

The Lord has guaranteed "not to abandon you nor send you away in your old age. He won't abandon you when your strength and power are exhausted ". "For on the day of adversity, He will conceal you in His shelter.

He will place you atop a lofty rock. Even though your earthly parent, mother, and friends may abandon you when you need them most, the Lord will welcome you as His child " (Psalm 27:5, 10).

The fear of Ebola and other viruses and diseases fills many individuals with fear. In contrast, "those who know their God will be strong and do exploits" (Daniel 11:32), and the Lord will remove disease from them (Deuteronomy 7:15).

"He will deliver them from the fowler's snare and the fearful plague. You should not fear the fear by night, the arrows that fly by day, the pestilence that lurks in the night, or the destruction and quick death that surprises at midday.

"It may fall a thousand to your left and ten thousand to your right, but it won't approach you. Because you have made the Lord your sanctuary and the Highest your abode, you will just be a spectator." (Psalm 91:3-16).

Dear reader, Today, the Lord says to you: Don't be afraid because I am with you; don't stare around in panic and fear, for I am your God. I will fortify you and make you resistant to adversity; I will assist you; I will support and maintain you with My right hand. I am the Lord who tells you not to be afraid; I will assist you! (Isaiah 41:10-13).

These are the promises of God under such circumstances, and He will never allow you to mistrust Him, only that you have faith in His message and have no fear. "Even when the chains of grief encircle you and death's horror grips you, call upon the name of the Lord, and He will release you from all of them." "Because His mercy and lovingkindness are great toward us and the Lord's truth and fidelity endure forever" (Psalm 117:2).

You and your family may be burdened by misery and sorrow, but in the name of Jesus, you will eliminate them! The Lord will raise you and make you stand if illness brings you down. "You shall not die but live. " To proclaim the kindness and mighty acts of the Lord throughout the land of the living (Psalm 118:17). It is that you have no fear!

Are you still frightened? Then have faith in the Lord since He never fails. His words are you and Amen, and He has remained unchanged yesterday, today, and forever (Malachi 3:6; Hebrews 13:8).

His grace will sustain you in life's raging storm; he will guide you through the valley of shadows and carry you across life's turbulent sea, and it is my prayer that when the doorway to eternal life opens, neither you nor I will be absent from the Book of Life (a record), so that we may enter with the Lord.

Paul's message to the church in Rome speaks to us all that "the sufferings of this present time are not worth comparing to the glory that will be revealed to us, in us and for us," whose hope is based solely on the blood and righteousness of Jesus.

Nothing will separate us from Christ's love, even in these circumstances. "Will there be a hardship, affliction, and tribulation? Or catastrophe and misery? Or persecution, starvation, danger, or the sword? As it is written. Yet amid all these things, we are more than conquerors, gaining an overwhelming victory through Him who loves us " (Romans 8:18-37).

CHAPTER 12: IF YOU DON'T MAINTAIN YOUR FAITH, YOU WON'T STAND AT ALL.

When the Bible mentions faith, it doesn't relate to faith in a particular religion or ministry. In the Bible, faith always refers to trust in God and His power. This is the only faith that God will accept.

The kingdoms of Aram and Israel marched toward Jerusalem to defeat King Ahaz of Judah. Their effort was futile. However, they were not content with their defeat. They acquired a new ally in Ephraim and strengthened their position. When this news reached Ahaz and his people, they were so afraid that they trembled "like the trees in the forest."

Although Ahaz was not an exemplary monarch, God did not abandon him and his people to their anxieties. He dispatched Isaiah and his son to meet them and advise them to be cautious, cool, and fearless. God instructed them not to be disheartened by the "firewood."

That is how God perceives the enemy. He may arrive to fill our hearts with fear. He may try to terrify us by issuing threats, but God sees him as nothing more than fuel for His eternal fire. When the enemy attempts to frighten us, may we remember what he is in God's eyes? He is little compared to the awe-inspiring power of the creator of the universe.

God gives us victory against our adversary. May we learn to view threats from God's viewpoint rather than our own. May we learn to focus on the win rather than the enemy's strategies. In Psalm 58:9, God guarantees that the wicked will be swept away before they can truly harm His people, and in retrospect, our concerns were unwarranted.

God instructs Ahaz to observe whom these foes worship. They place their confidence and trust in a man with only a breath in his nostrils. In what regard is he? They've made guys their priority. They submit to the flesh's wisdom and notions.

The "head" of Ahaz is the God of the heavenly army. Those individuals have no chance against Him. God mercifully calms Ahaz and his people's concerns by assuring them, "It won't occur; it won't occur."

Their bombastic threats and arrogant schemes will have no effect whatsoever. In formulating their schemes for devastation, they have omitted the most significant variable, namely God. They have made arrangements, but nothing will result from this. No intelligence, perception, or strategy can prevail against the Lord.

However, Ahaz found it difficult to believe God's words. Even after receiving words of comfort from God directly through His prophet Isaiah, the threat of the enemy still overwhelmed him. God tells him to cling to his trust in God despite his uncertainties. He says, "If your faith is not strong, you won't stand at all." Without faith, pleasing God is impossible.

Let our trust not be shaken whenever a new obstacle arises. This is what the Israelites did while they traveled through the desert. Every time they encountered a new difficulty, they questioned whether God would assist them. "When He hit the rock, water burst forth, and many streams flowed, but can He provide us with food? Can He give His people with meat?" (Psalm 78:20).

The psalmist continues by stating that God was angry with them for their lack of trust. God had to demonstrate His steadfastness every time they encountered a new difficulty. With each new obstacle, they questioned His capacity. They provoked Him because they lacked faith in God and confidence in His deliverance. (Psalm 78:22).

We don't live in the past, but remembering prior wins strengthens our faith when confronting new obstacles (see Psalm 77:9-14). May these musings strengthen our faith in God so that we may believe that He who stated, "The Egyptians you see today, you will never see again" (Exodus 14:13), will respond similarly to every new enemy danger.

The most recent difficulty may be novel to us, but nothing surprises God. May we maintain our stability so that we don't slip and fall. May we remain steadfast in our faith regardless of our new obstacles.

CHAPTER 13: DON'T LET FEAR HINDER OR STOP YOUR DREAM.

Fear is the greatest impediment to a person's goals and potential. If we don't control fear, it will master us, causing us to stay when we should go, stop when we should move, remain silent when we should speak, and delay when we should act. Fear is lethal. Fear of "what if" prevents many people from doing what they know in their hearts could and should be done, and fear lacks regard for others.

Someone once remarked, "Fear is false evidence presenting itself as genuine." This is a fantastic example of how fear binds people to mediocrity and cowardice, making them captives. It aims to obstruct and thwart those who believe in their dreams and strive for achievement.

Fear is a force, an unseen power that must be considered. Fear prevents us from taking risks and pursuing our goals. Fear prevents us from giving that speech, singing, or writing a book. However, fear may be overcome.

God never intended for us to walk in fear, for fear causes suffering. When we can't do what our hearts desire, we experience sadness and regret. Consider the matter carefully.

What if someone born to sing can't express themselves because they are terrified of what others may think of their voice?

What if a person destined to write books never does so out of fear of failure?

Suppose a person born to speak in some capacity (inspirational speeches, motivational speaking, or preaching and teaching the Bible) refrains from doing so out of fear of making a mistake. Then the recipient will live a miserable life.

Why do you ask? The answer is that when a person is born to do or be something, he or she won't feel whole until that route is pursued and appreciated.

Birds are designed for flight. Fishes are designed for swimming. It is intuitive for them. They were designed to perform their functions effectively.

Similarly, it is only when you and I discover what we were born to do and pursue it persistently, refusing to bow to that awful thing called fear, that we experience true freedom of expression for our heart's desire and our souls enter a state of "holy rapture," rejoicing in the fact that we are doing what we love to do and feeling fulfilled in life.

Fear should never prevent you from pursuing your objectives. Yes, you can experience fear but do what you know to be necessary regardless of your emotions.

When you overcome your anxieties with a determined effort to be who you want to be, do what you want to do, and own what you want to possess, you will discover that fear can never prevent you from being a winner since it can be overcome and is no match for a person of faith.

Is faith required for success and triumph in achieving our objectives? Yes, absolutely. With the power and spiritual force bestowed upon us by the Creator, we may overcome fear and triumph.

So have faith in your dream. Believe that you can reach them with God's help. Then proceed. Take persistently courageous and relentless action. Ignore these fears and emotions of inadequacy. Follow your knowledge. Keep at it. You were born to succeed.

CHAPTER 14: HAVE FAITH IN GOD.

From the very beginning of the Bible, there is one persistent theme: God's enormous love and compassion for us. He desires our success. In his immutability, we can place a great deal of confidence. There appears to be no greater motivation for faith than the knowledge that God is totally on our side.

When we realize that He has called us to success, it is easier to have faith in our ability to achieve our mission and destiny on Earth.

God's love for us is so great that He sent Jesus to die for us, willingly exchanging His life for ours. He did so fully aware of the terrible cost to Himself. He loves us beyond our ability to grasp and has provided us with wonderful blessings through the Covenant. Even under the Old Covenant, He warned us not to forget His blessings. Thanks to God!

Psalms 103:2 Bless the Lord, my soul, and don't forget all of His benefits: 3. Who forgives all your transgressions, Who heals all your sicknesses, 4. Who redeems your life from destruction, Who crowns you with lovingkindness and delicate mercies, 5. Who fills your mouth with good things, so your youth is renewed like an eagle.

Have we forgotten, or did we simply never believe?

In any case, the body of Christ is being shaken in a manner unprecedented in history. In a world filled with disorder, it is simple to stray from the path God has laid out for us.

Currently, the world appears to be in disarray, and all that is occurring can appear overwhelming. In the midst of this, each of us must make a decision. We must determine whether God's love for us is genuine. God's love is always demonstrated via action, but man's understanding of love is sometimes empty words.

How do we know that God loves us if we are not experiencing its benefits? Initially, the action has already occurred. Jesus completed the mission for which He was sent. To please God, regardless of where we came from, requires trust.

There is no possible way around this. If we have never been instructed in His promises, we can't have the trust necessary to walk in them, for faith always stems from knowing God's will. If we are unaware of His promises, we have no basis on which to believe.

We must know God's promises to walk in them by faith, no? Jesus spoke the same thing in John 8:32 you will know the truth, and it will set you free. Knowing that God is on our side is essential to having faith that He will demonstrate His favor toward us. Knowing Him is knowing the truth because He is the truth.

So many view God as their adversary rather than their savior, and they choose to flee from Him rather than to Him. He is the One who holds the answers, is an ever-present assistant in times of need, and has freely given us everything.

Many have been instructed on how God purifies us by putting us through every unpleasant circumstance. Only the blood of Jesus Christ can purify us. I know sanctification is a process, but the job has already been accomplished. There is no point in trying to gain it on our own, as it is impossible. Our task is to believe in Him. As we believe in Him, righteousness will reveal itself in and through us.

Romans 4:2 If Abraham were justified by his works, he would have something to boast about but not before God. For what does the Bible state? "Because Abraham believed in God, he was recognized as righteous." Now, salaries are not viewed as grace but as debt for the worker. 5. But anyone who doesn't work but believes in Him who justifies the ungodly, his faith is considered as righteousness.

You can assert that I have never experienced God's goodness in my life. If this is the case, understand that you must first seek Him.

Genesis 12:2 focuses on Jesus, the originator, and perfecter of our faith.

If you are just focusing on the negative aspects of your life, you are looking at the wrong things. You must turn away from the things you are currently observing and begin to observe the proper objects. Commence by worshipping Him. Provide Him with material to work with. Faith is always appreciative and always glorifies God. You can't complain and have faith at the same time.

Examine yourself. Decide to be grateful even if your circumstances indicate that you are failing and have little hope of ever succeeding. God can't work on your side if you constantly grumble and moan. You certainly won't if you refuse to turn to Christ Jesus' constant, victorious agent.

You are praising Him for His protection, deliverance, and perfect faithfulness, not for all the negative things occurring. He never has and will never fail. If we wish to walk in this victory, we must walk with Him.

Faith is what pleases Him, and praise is the trigger that stimulates faith; this is evident throughout the Bible. Learn to rely on Him and observe His total fidelity. This is a lifestyle, not a recipe.

God resides in the adoration of His people. (Psalms 22:3.) Alternately, one could say that God reveals Himself via the praises of His people. He is an active, alive God who wants to demonstrate His strength on our behalf.

Psalms 34:1 I will continually bless the Lord and sing His praise.

David received a vision of God's immense love for him. He had great conviction in it. He had no qualms in turning to Him regardless of the circumstances. David repeatedly returned to Him and rested in His tremendous love despite committing many mistakes.

No wonder God declared him to be a man after His own heart. Even when our activities result in undesirable outcomes, we may and should still turn to the One who has all the answers and will show us the way out.

I have learned from my experience that when I look to Him, I will obtain the answers I need to escape any issue. It is virtually never the escape route you would have selected, but it is the route to safety that only God can provide.

He is the One who can restore us and direct us to triumph. I am certain that because He has done it for me, He will also do it for you. Learn to have absolute and complete faith in Him. Say this with me: If God is on my side, who can oppose me?

As this thinking develops within you, you will reach heights you never imagined possible. Let Him reveal His tremendous love to you and behold the Lord's deliverance.

Ephesians chapter 2 verse 4: God, abundant in kindness, has shown us mercy because of His great love for us.

Our religion should be founded on His immense love for us. So many Christians put faith in their faith rather than the One who is the author and perfecter of our faith. The greater your understanding of Him, the greater your love for Him.

The greater your love for Him, the greater your faith in Him. The greater your trust in Him, the greater your faith. It is all interconnected. It becomes simpler when you walk in complete trust and assurance, knowing God is on your side and not against us. This may be improved; we must all progress in this area.

Don't be frightened of making mistakes, as this only leads to the things you fear. According to His Word, perfect love casts away all fear. Even if you make a mistake, you can be assured that He will restore you and show you how to go back on course. This calms a great deal of pressure.

1 John 4:18 There is no fear in love; pure love dispels fear because fear implies suffering. However, he who worries has not yet achieved perfection in love.

I consider this wonderful news. My faith is not in my abilities but in God alone. As we trust Him and walk in pure love, we become perfected and lose our fear of failing.

Do we believe in our capacity for faith?

This allows us to reduce religion to a formula. Our faith is in Someone, not stuff. Someone who the Bible says can't fail. We can take great comfort in believing He will never disappoint us. Ultimately, He is the One who will fulfill His promises.

Numbers 23:19 "God is neither a man, who would lie nor a descendant of man, who would repent. Has He spoken, but will He not act? Or, if He has spoken, will He not fulfill it? God can't deceive and can't fail in any way. When received, this fact is life-changing. We can take comfort in this. We should be confident but place all our confidence in Him.

According to (James 4), true humility is not self-effacement but putting one's total reliance on God. A humble attitude will prevent failure. James stated that

God bestows more grace upon the meek. This enables Him to grant you more grace than you already have, and we need all the grace we can obtain.

Grace is granted to accomplish His desire. This occurs when we turn to Him and place our complete trust in Him. Our faith won't rest in our abilities or anointing but in Him, who anoints us. See the distinction?

Mark 11:22 So Jesus responded and told them: "Put your trust in God.

This may sound apparent, but a great number of Christians put their faith in everything but God. Occasionally, this occurs within their church or with other clergy or ministries. Men can fail, but God can't. Where do you stand if your faith is in a guy or ministry and they fail?

All of us should be praying for those ministers who have failed somehow. We are often dependent on their success. Everyone is in this together. Their success and failure are often the same as ours.

We require one another. Nevertheless, we must lay our faith solely in God. We must have confidence, but it must be in the unshakeable truth of God and His Word, not in ourselves or the abilities of others. We have no powers except those He has granted us.

Jesus continued by saying. Verse 23 "For surely, I say to you, whoever says to this mountain, "Be removed and cast into the sea," and believes in his heart that what he says will occur, will have whatever he says. 24 "Therefore, I say to you, whatever you ask for in prayer, believe that you have received it and will receive it.

As Jesus said, we should have trust and believe our words. We must have trust that our words will come to pass, but He first instructed us to have faith in God. Unlike us, he did not get the sequence of things confused. Our faith is either in God or in the words we speak.

If our faith is in God and the unwavering truth of His Word, then we may also be certain that our own words will come to pass. This is possible because our words and faith are founded in Him and the unchanging truth of His Word. Amen

CONCLUSION.

Everyone has at least one phobia. The only variation is how it impacts various lives and how much power we give it. God is always willing to assist us since He knows our human frailties. God has repeatedly offered help, regardless of whether a person's fear is deeply established, resembles a dark dungeon, or is only partly conscious. How can we obtain this help?

The initial step is to acknowledge that the fear that paralyzes and prevents one from performing at one's best is not from God. 2 Timothy 1:7 states that God has not given us a spirit of fear. If it is not from God, one must refuse to accept it. The spirit of fear comes from Satan. He is concerned about stealing, murdering, and destroying whatever makes the victim's life enjoyable. - John 10:10

Knowing the truth is what sets one free - John 8:32. In enlisting God's help, there is a fact that you must recognize with your entire mind and being. Genesis

1:26 states that we are identical to the Lord God. God made us in his likeness and image and endowed us with abilities commensurate with our divine essence. One of the ways to access this divine nature is faith.

Knowledge is insufficient if it is not supported by belief and faith. Unleash your faith based on the Bible; what has God said in circumstances where He anticipated a person's fear? -Isaiah 40:10, Joshua 1:10. Let go of control and have faith.

Daniel 3:17 and 18. Strive to reach the point of faith that God will offer protection from the repercussions of what the fear portends, and if He doesn't, so be it. Absolute trust and serene assurance in God's will for one's life both lessen and eradicate all fears.

Meditations on God's promises about our anxieties instill confidence, calm, and assurance. Proclaim the promises to yourself; speak the word to yourself. Remind God in the prayer of His words and promises. Isaiah1:18a.

Make a decision; address your anxieties by taking a step of faith. James 4:7 states, "Resist the adversary (fear), and he will depart." Be patient with yourself and, having done everything possible, stand; be confident that God has heard your prayers and declaration. Your spirit is indeed bolstered to deal with the current circumstance.

As you pray, grasp the promises surrounding fear and refuse to embrace Satan's falsehood. Communicate and reflect upon the Word. Faith would eventually displace fear. Fear is a spirit; entertaining fear is equivalent to welcoming an unwelcome houseguest. Remember that the Holy Spirit can't reside there if fear rules your life. Light and darkness are incompatible.

This book is part of an ongoing collection called "Spiritual Attraction."

- ➢ Ask Believe Receive.
- ➢ Faith Like a Mustard Seed.
- ➢ You Were Made for Such a Time as This.
- ➢ Let Go and Just Let God Handle it for You.
- ➢ You Have Not Because You Ask Not.
- ➢ Not my Will Lord but Let Your Will be Done.
- ➢ Asking for This or Something Better.
- ➢ What is your Why.
- ➢ God said 365 Times in the Bible; DO NOT BE AFRAID.
- ➢ 10, 100, and 1,000 Fold Increase.
- ➢ Immeasurable More than I Hope or Imagine.
- ➢ All Things are Possible, If you Believe.

Other Series by Sherry Lee

"Laws of the Universe"

- ➢ Law of Assumption.

"Opening and Balancing Your Chakra's"

- ➢ Unblocking your 3rd Eye
- ➢ Opening and Balancing your Heart Chakra
- ➢ Opening and Balancing your Crown Chakra
- ➢ Opening and Balancing your Throat Chakra
- ➢ Opening and Balancing your Solar Plexu Chakra
- ➢ Opening and Balancing your Sacral Chakra
- ➢ Opening and Balancing your Root Chakra.

"Why Alternative Medicine Works"

- ➢ Why Yoga Works
- ➢ Why Chakra Works
- ➢ Why Massage Therapy Works
- ➢ Why Reflexology Works
- ➢ Why Acupuncture Works
- ➢ Why Reiki Works
- ➢ Why Meditation Works
- ➢ Why Hypnosis Works
- ➢ Why Colon Cleansing Works
- ➢ Why NLP (Neuro Linguistic Programming) Works
- ➢ Why Energy Healing Works
- ➢ Why Foot Detoxing Works
- ➢ Why Singing Bowls Works.

- ➢ Why Tapping Works
- ➢ Why Muscle Testing Works.

"Using Sage and Smudging"

- ➢ Learning About Sage and Smudging
- ➢ Sage and Smudging for Love
- ➢ Sage and Smudging for Health and Healing
- ➢ Sage and Smudging for Wealth and Abundance
- ➢ Sage and Smudging for Spiritual Cleansing
- ➢ Sage and Smudging for Negativity.

"Learning About Crystals"

- ➢ Crystals for Love
- ➢ Crystals for Health
- ➢ Crystals for Wealth
- ➢ Crystals for Spiritual Cleansing
- ➢ Crystals for Removing Negativity.

"What Every Newlywed Should Know and Discuss Before Marriage."

> ➢ Newlywed Communication on Money
> ➢ Newlywed Communication on In-laws
> ➢ Newlywed Communication about Children.
> ➢ Newlywed Communication on Religion.
> ➢ Newlywed Communication on Friends.
> ➢ Newlywed Communication on Retirement.
> ➢ Newlywed Communication on Sex.
> ➢ Newlywed Communication on Boundaries.
> ➢ Newlywed Communication on Roles and Responsibilities.

"Health is Wealth."

> ➢ Health is Wealth
> ➢ Positivity is Wealth
> ➢ Emotions is Wealth.
> ➢ Social Health is Wealth.
> ➢ Happiness is Wealth.
> ➢ Fitness is Wealth.
> ➢ Meditating is Wealth.
> ➢ Communication is Wealth.
> ➢ Mental Health is Wealth.
> ➢ Gratitude is Wealth.

"Personal Development Collection."

> Manifesting for Beginners
> Crystals for Beginners
> How to Manifest More Money into your Life.
> How to work from home more effectively.
> How to Accomplish more in Less Time.
> How to End Procrastination.
> Learning to Praise and acknowledge your Accomplishments.
> How to Become your Own Driving Force.
> Creating a Confident Persona.
> How to Meditate.
> How to Set Affirmations.
> How to Set and Achieve your Goals.
> Achieving Your Fitness Goals.
> Achieving Your Weight Loss Goals.
> How to Create an Effective Vision Board.

Other Books By Sherry Lee:

> Repeating Angel Numbers
> Most Popular Archangels.

Author Bio

Sherry Lee. Sherry enjoys reading personal development books, so she decided to write about something she is passionate about. More books will come in this collection, so follow her on Amazon for more books.

Thank you for your purchase of this book.

I honestly do appreciate it and appreciate you, my excellent customer.

God Bless You.

Sherry Lee.

11841237R00064